Turtles have similar tough shells to shield themselves in the same way against sea birds, crabs and large fish.
 A hedgehog tucks its head against its soft furry belly close to its feet and rolls into a prickly ball. One touch of its sharp spines is enough to stop other animals from hurting it.

Lobsters and crabs have hard crusty shells and sharp claws for protection. They also scuttle away into narrow cracks in rocks to hide from their enemies. Shellfish are well-named and well-protected. Like crabs, some kinds can shelter among rocks, while others dig deep down into sand, where they are out of sight and out of reach.

A snail draws its soft body right back inside its shell to hide from hungry birds.

Survival Skills

Contents	Page
Shells and spikes	2-5
Skunk and octopus	6-7
Ducks	8-9
Cats and other animals	10-11
Fighting back	12-13
Flying fish	14-15
Butterflies	16-17
Blending in	18-19
Escaping	20-21
Noisy warnings	22-23
Index	24

written by Pam Holden

Tough shells

Animals have developed many different methods to avoid danger and defend themselves from threats. Some creatures carry their own simple protection with them on their backs at all times: a tortoise can withdraw its head and legs under its hard thick shell, where it cannot be reached by a hungry eagle or snake.

Squirting and spraying

A skunk in trouble sprays a horrible smelly liquid (musk) all over attackers to turn them away. The nasty stink lasts for several days, teaching the skunk's enemy a lesson it won't ever forget! An octopus reacts to an attack by squirting a cloud of thick black ink around itself. This acts like a screen, so that its enemy can't see it escaping in the murky water. By the time the black liquid clears, the octopus is safely out of range in a special hiding spot.

Pretending

When a mother duck senses danger for her young, she leads the attacker away by pretending she has a broken wing: she flies slowly away from the nest, dragging one wing and quacking loudly. She wants the hungry enemy to think she is injured and therefore will be easy to catch. She hopes it will follow her instead of finding her nest with her eggs or helpless baby ducklings. If it gets too close, she flies quickly away and hides until she can return safely to her babies.

Cats arch their backs and fluff up their fur, hissing and spitting at their attackers, which are often dogs. Bears usually walk on four legs, but when frightened they rear up on their two hind legs to make themselves look bigger and more threatening.

A bittern is a large brown bird which protects itself by pretending to be a stick. It puts its beak high up in the air and freezes, standing absolutely still among the bushes in the shape of a stick, or sometimes even swaying in the breeze.

Fighting back

Many animals have a special way to fight back by hurting their attackers: some carry "built-in" defensive weapons with which they kick, bite, claw or use sharp horns when under attack.
Others such as bees, wasps, scorpions, stingrays and jellyfish all have sharp stings to injure their enemies.
Some snakes spit poison into their attacker's eyes; others hiss or bite. Alpacas and camels spit when they feel threatened.

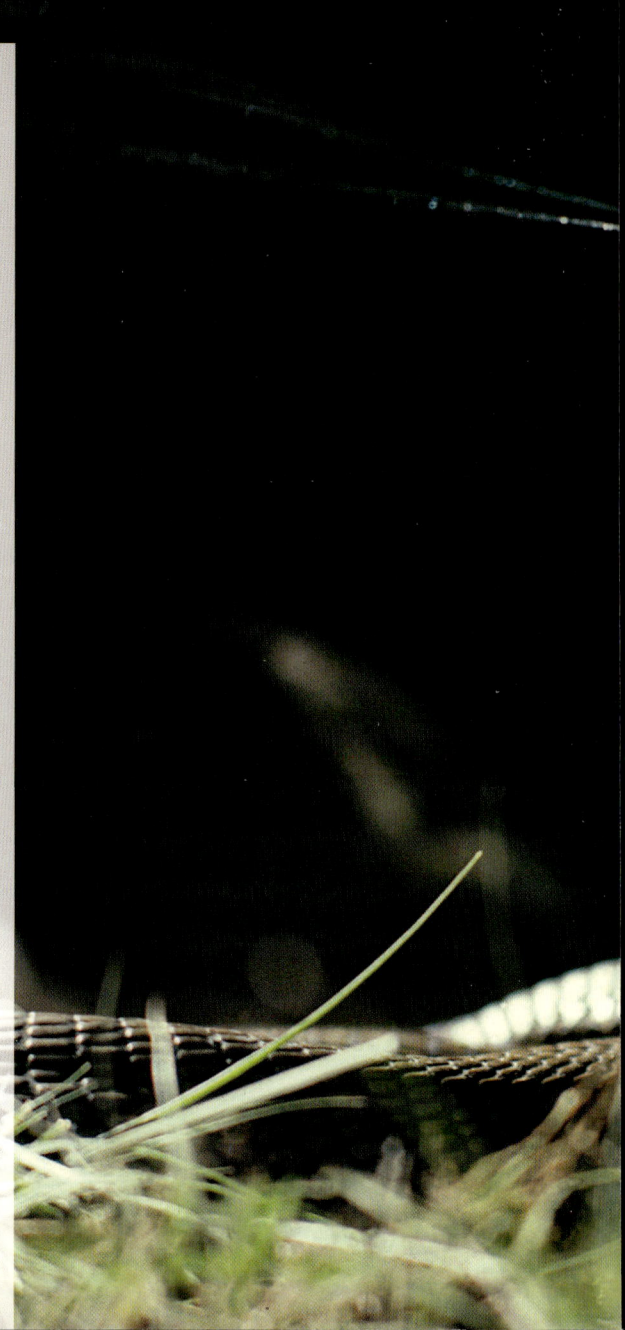

spitting cobra

Can fish fly?

In the sea there is one type of fish that has an amazing escape route: flying fish leap right out of the water to flee from predators like sharks. They can glide through the air on their wing-like fins at speeds up to 43 miles/ 70 km per hour. When they sometimes land on a boat deck, their fate depends whether the crew members are kind or hungry!

flying fish

Nasty taste

Butterflies and some other insects are brightly patterned for good reason: after one bad experience with a ghastly meal, hungry birds remember that bright insects taste horrid, so they leave them alone.

Clever camouflage!

Camouflage is used by creatures that want to blend into their environment so that they are hard to see. A well-known example is the zebra, whose black and white stripes are very difficult to see against sunlit wavy grass. Some lizards called chameleons can change like a rainbow to match different surroundings. Stick insects have long thin bodies shaped just like twigs, so that hungry birds don't see them on branches.

Speedy escapes

Fast-moving animals have safe hiding places that can be reached quickly: e.g. rodents hide in holes; rabbits race to burrows; birds fly into trees. Dark caves are used by bears, foxes, bats and birds.
A frog never goes far from its home – a pond or stream. With its long back legs it leaps away from birds or cats to the safety of the water.

bullfrog

Warning

Messages are sent to warn others of danger: apes beat their chests like drums; elephants trumpet loudly; kangaroos, rabbits and frogs stamp heavily on the ground with their strong hind legs; birds squawk loudly as they fly away; beavers slap the water surface with their hard flat tails. All the world's creatures need smart skills to survive.

Index	**Page**
claws	4-5, 12
liquid spray	6-7
noises	8, 22-23
octopus	6
shields	2-5
speedy escape	14-15, 20-21
spits	10, 12-13
stings	12
threats	10, 12-13
tricks	8, 10-11, 16, 18-19
weapons	12